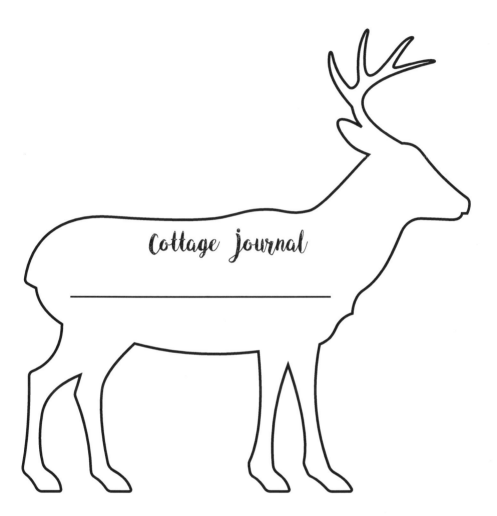

Cottage Journal

## Date

## Weather

## Projects

## Friends

## Adventures & Memories

## To Do

## Wildlife Encounters

## Date

## Weather

## Projects

## Friends

## Adventures & Memories

## To Do

## Wildlife Encounters

Date

Weather

Projects

Friends

Adventures & Memories

To Do

Wildlife Encounters

## Date

## Weather

## Projects

## Friends

## Adventures & Memories

## To Do

## Wildlife Encounters

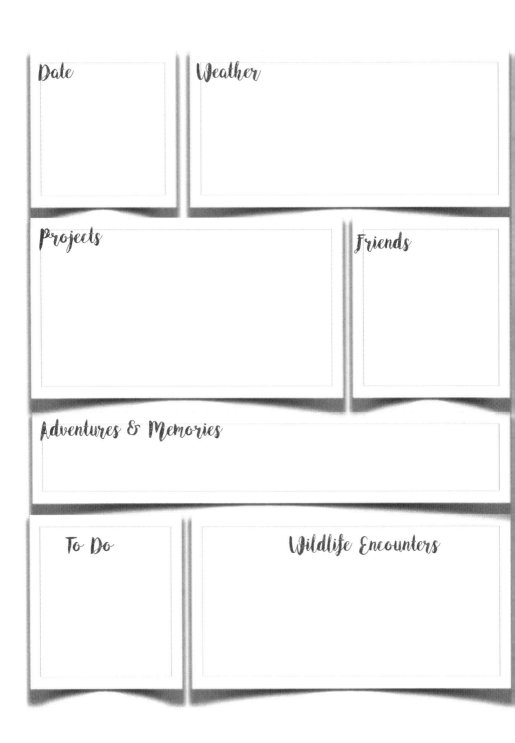

Date

Weather

Projects

Friends

Adventures & Memories

To Do

Wildlife Encounters

## Date

## Weather

## Projects

## Friends

## Adventures & Memories

## To Do

## Wildlife Encounters

## Date

## Weather

## Projects

## Friends

## Adventures & Memories

## To Do

## Wildlife Encounters

## Date

## Weather

## Projects

## Friends

## Adventures & Memories

## To Do

## Wildlife Encounters

Date

Weather

Projects

Friends

Adventures & Memories

To Do

Wildlife Encounters

## Date

## Weather

## Projects

## Friends

## Adventures & Memories

## To Do

## Wildlife Encounters

Date

Weather

Projects

Friends

Adventures & Memories

To Do

Wildlife Encounters

## Date

## Weather

## Projects

## Friends

## Adventures & Memories

## To Do

## Wildlife Encounters

## Date

## Weather

## Projects

## Friends

## Adventures & Memories

## To Do

## Wildlife Encounters

## Date

## Weather

## Projects

## Friends

## Adventures & Memories

## To Do

## Wildlife Encounters

## Date

## Weather

## Projects

## Friends

## Adventures & Memories

## To Do

## Wildlife Encounters

## Date

## Weather

## Projects

## Friends

## Adventures & Memories

## To Do

## Wildlife Encounters

## Date

## Weather

## Projects

## Friends

## Adventures & Memories

## To Do

## Wildlife Encounters

Date

Weather

Projects

Friends

Adventures & Memories

To Do

Wildlife Encounters

Date

Weather

Projects

Friends

Adventures & Memories

To Do

Wildlife Encounters

# Date

# Weather

# Projects

# Friends

# Adventures & Memories

# To Do

# Wildlife Encounters

## Date

## Weather

## Projects

## Friends

## Adventures & Memories

## To Do

## Wildlife Encounters

## Date

## Weather

## Projects

## Friends

## Adventures & Memories

## To Do

## Wildlife Encounters

Date

Weather

Projects

Friends

Adventures & Memories

To Do

Wildlife Encounters

## Date

## Weather

## Projects

## Friends

## Adventures & Memories

## To Do

## Wildlife Encounters

Date

Weather

Projects

Friends

Adventures & Memories

To Do

Wildlife Encounters

## Date

## Weather

## Projects

## Friends

## Adventures & Memories

## To Do

## Wildlife Encounters

Date

Weather

Projects

Friends

Adventures & Memories

To Do

Wildlife Encounters

# Date

# Weather

# Projects

# Friends

# Adventures & Memories

# To Do

# Wildlife Encounters

Date

Weather

Projects

Friends

Adventures & Memories

To Do

Wildlife Encounters

Date

Weather

Projects

Friends

Adventures & Memories

To Do

Wildlife Encounters

Date

Weather

Projects

Friends

Adventures & Memories

To Do

Wildlife Encounters

Date

Weather

Projects

Friends

Adventures & Memories

To Do

Wildlife Encounters

## Date

## Weather

## Projects

## Friends

## Adventures & Memories

## To Do

## Wildlife Encounters

Date

Weather

Projects

Friends

Adventures & Memories

To Do

Wildlife Encounters

# Date

# Weather

# Projects

# Friends

# Adventures & Memories

# To Do

# Wildlife Encounters

Date

Weather

Projects

Friends

Adventures & Memories

To Do

Wildlife Encounters

## Date

## Weather

## Projects

## Friends

## Adventures & Memories

## To Do

## Wildlife Encounters

## Date

## Weather

## Projects

## Friends

## Adventures & Memories

## To Do

## Wildlife Encounters

Date

Weather

Projects

Friends

Adventures & Memories

To Do

Wildlife Encounters

Date

Weather

Projects

Friends

Adventures & Memories

To Do

Wildlife Encounters

## Date

## Weather

## Projects

## Friends

## Adventures & Memories

## To Do

## Wildlife Encounters

Date

Weather

Projects

Friends

Adventures & Memories

To Do

Wildlife Encounters

## Date

## Weather

## Projects

## Friends

## Adventures & Memories

## To Do

## Wildlife Encounters

## Date

## Weather

## Projects

## Friends

## Adventures & Memories

## To Do

## Wildlife Encounters

## Date

## Weather

## Projects

## Friends

## Adventures & Memories

## To Do

## Wildlife Encounters

Date

Weather

Projects

Friends

Adventures & Memories

To Do

Wildlife Encounters

## Date

## Weather

## Projects

## Friends

## Adventures & Memories

## To Do

## Wildlife Encounters

Date

Weather

Projects

Friends

Adventures & Memories

To Do

Wildlife Encounters

Date

Weather

Projects

Friends

Adventures & Memories

To Do

Wildlife Encounters

# Date

# Weather

# Projects

# Friends

# Adventures & Memories

# To Do

# Wildlife Encounters

Date

Weather

Projects

Friends

Adventures & Memories

To Do

Wildlife Encounters

# Date

# Weather

# Projects

# Friends

# Adventures & Memories

# To Do

# Wildlife Encounters

## Date

## Weather

## Projects

## Friends

## Adventures & Memories

## To Do

## Wildlife Encounters

Date

Weather

Projects

Friends

Adventures & Memories

To Do

Wildlife Encounters

# Date

# Weather

# Projects

# Friends

# Adventures & Memories

# To Do

# Wildlife Encounters

## Date

## Weather

## Projects

## Friends

## Adventures & Memories

## To Do

## Wildlife Encounters

Date

Weather

Projects

Friends

Adventures & Memories

To Do

Wildlife Encounters

Date

Weather

Projects

Friends

Adventures & Memories

To Do

Wildlife Encounters

Date

Weather

Projects

Friends

Adventures & Memories

To Do

Wildlife Encounters

## Date

## Weather

## Projects

## Friends

## Adventures & Memories

## To Do

## Wildlife Encounters

Date

Weather

Projects

Friends

Adventures & Memories

To Do

Wildlife Encounters

Date

Weather

Projects

Friends

Adventures & Memories

To Do

Wildlife Encounters

## Date

## Weather

## Projects

## Friends

## Adventures & Memories

## To Do

## Wildlife Encounters

Date

Weather

Projects

Friends

Adventures & Memories

To Do

Wildlife Encounters

Date

Weather

Projects

Friends

Adventures & Memories

To Do

Wildlife Encounters

Date

Weather

Projects

Friends

Adventures & Memories

To Do

Wildlife Encounters

Date

Weather

Projects

Friends

Adventures & Memories

To Do

Wildlife Encounters

Date

Weather

Projects

Friends

Adventures & Memories

To Do

Wildlife Encounters

## Date

## Weather

## Projects

## Friends

## Adventures & Memories

## To Do

## Wildlife Encounters

# Date

# Weather

# Projects

# Friends

# Adventures & Memories

# To Do

# Wildlife Encounters

Date

Weather

Projects

Friends

Adventures & Memories

To Do

Wildlife Encounters

Date

Weather

Projects

Friends

Adventures & Memories

To Do

Wildlife Encounters

Date

Weather

Projects

Friends

Adventures & Memories

To Do

Wildlife Encounters

Date

Weather

Projects

Friends

Adventures & Memories

To Do

Wildlife Encounters

Date

Weather

Projects

Friends

Adventures & Memories

To Do

Wildlife Encounters

Date

Weather

Projects

Friends

Adventures & Memories

To Do

Wildlife Encounters

Date

Weather

Projects

Friends

Adventures & Memories

To Do

Wildlife Encounters

Date

Weather

Projects

Friends

Adventures & Memories

To Do

Wildlife Encounters

## Date

## Weather

## Projects

## Friends

## Adventures & Memories

## To Do

## Wildlife Encounters

## Date

## Weather

## Projects

## Friends

## Adventures & Memories

## To Do

## Wildlife Encounters

Date

Weather

Projects

Friends

Adventures & Memories

To Do

Wildlife Encounters

Date

Weather

Projects

Friends

Adventures & Memories

To Do

Wildlife Encounters

Date

Weather

Projects

Friends

Adventures & Memories

To Do

Wildlife Encounters

Date

Weather

Projects

Friends

Adventures & Memories

To Do

Wildlife Encounters

Date

Weather

Projects

Friends

Adventures & Memories

To Do

Wildlife Encounters

## Date

## Weather

## Projects

## Friends

## Adventures & Memories

## To Do

## Wildlife Encounters

Date

Weather

Projects

Friends

Adventures & Memories

To Do

Wildlife Encounters

Date

Weather

Projects

Friends

Adventures & Memories

To Do

Wildlife Encounters

Date

Weather

Projects

Friends

Adventures & Memories

To Do

Wildlife Encounters

# Date

# Weather

# Projects

# Friends

# Adventures & Memories

# To Do

# Wildlife Encounters

Date

Weather

Projects

Friends

Adventures & Memories

To Do

Wildlife Encounters

Date

Weather

Projects

Friends

Adventures & Memories

To Do

Wildlife Encounters

Date

Weather

Projects

Friends

Adventures & Memories

To Do

Wildlife Encounters

Date

Weather

Projects

Friends

Adventures & Memories

To Do

Wildlife Encounters

Date

Weather

Projects

Friends

Adventures & Memories

To Do

Wildlife Encounters

Date

Weather

Projects

Friends

Adventures & Memories

To Do

Wildlife Encounters

## Date

## Weather

## Projects

## Friends

## Adventures & Memories

## To Do

## Wildlife Encounters

Date

Weather

Projects

Friends

Adventures & Memories

To Do

Wildlife Encounters

Date

Weather

Projects

Friends

Adventures & Memories

To Do

Wildlife Encounters

Date

Weather

Projects

Friends

Adventures & Memories

To Do

Wildlife Encounters

Date

Weather

Projects

Friends

Adventures & Memories

To Do

Wildlife Encounters

# Date

# Weather

# Projects

# Friends

# Adventures & Memories

# To Do

# Wildlife Encounters

Date

Weather

Projects

Friends

Adventures & Memories

To Do

Wildlife Encounters

# Important Cottage Information

# Important Cottage Information

# Important Cottage Information

# Important Cottage Information

# Important Cottage Information

# Important Cottage Information

Made in the USA
Middletown, DE
03 December 2019